Where I Live

My State

by Meg Gaertner

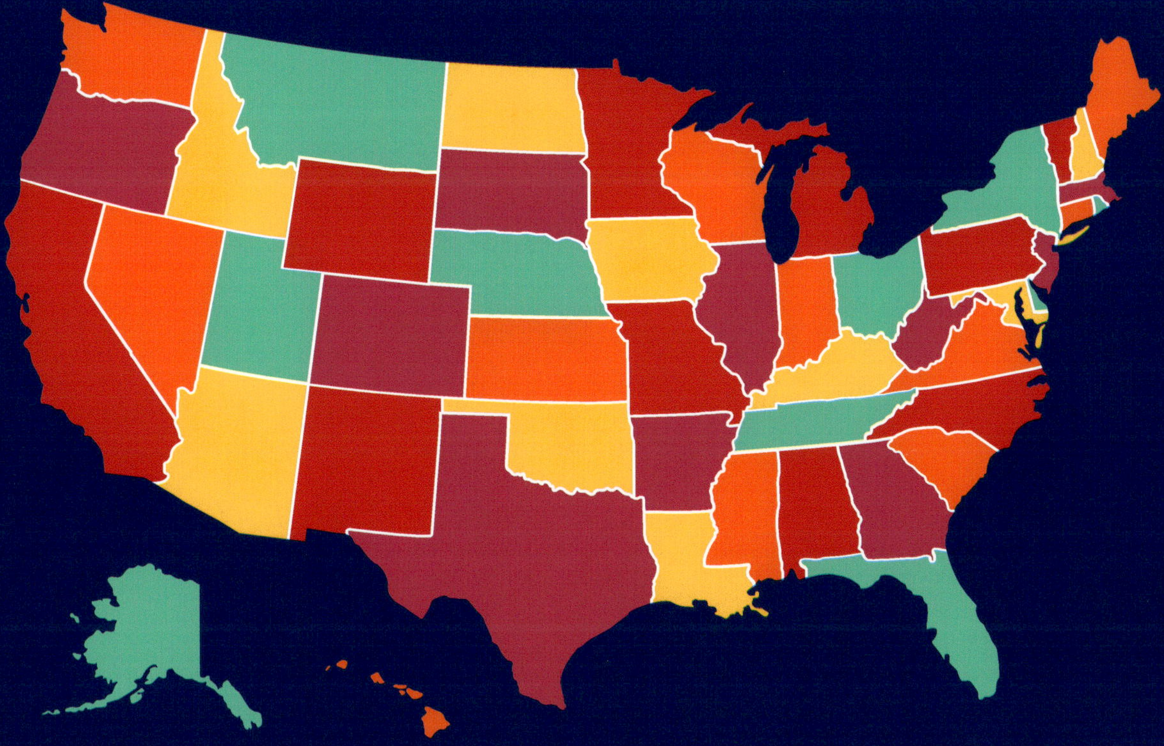

FOCUS READERS®
SCOUT

www.focusreaders.com

Focus Readers is distributed by North Star Editions:
sales@northstareditions.com | 888-417-0195

Produced for Focus Readers by Red Line Editorial.

Photographs ©: Shutterstock Images, cover, 1; iStockphoto, 4, 7 (top), 7 (bottom), 9, 11, 13 (top), 13 (bottom), 15, 16 (top left), 16 (bottom left), 16 (top right), 16 (bottom right)

Library of Congress Cataloging-in-Publication Data
Names: Gaertner, Meg, author.
Title: My state / Meg Gaertner.
Description: Lake Elmo, Minnesota : Focus Readers, [2021] | Series: Where I live | Includes index. | Audience: Grades K-1
Identifiers: LCCN 2019054822 (print) | LCCN 2019054823 (ebook) | ISBN 9781644933404 (Hardcover) | ISBN 9781644934166 (Paperback) | ISBN 9781644935682 (eBook PDF) | ISBN 9781644934920 (Hosted eBook)
Subjects: LCSH: U.S. states--Juvenile literature. | America--History--Juvenile literature. | Readers.
Classification: LCC E180 .G34 2021 (print) | LCC E180 (ebook) | DDC 973--dc23
LC record available at https://lccn.loc.gov/2019054822
LC ebook record available at https://lccn.loc.gov/2019054823

Printed in the United States of America
Mankato, MN
082020

About the Author

Meg Gaertner is a children's book editor and author. She lives in Minneapolis, Minnesota. When not writing, she is usually dancing or spending time outside.

Table of Contents

city
road
101
Los Angeles
5 NORTH
Sacramento
ONLY
10 WEST 5 SOUTH
Santa Monica
Santa Ana

In My State

I live in a state.

My state has many cities.

Long roads connect the cities.

People can move between cities.

They can drive a **car**.

They can take a **bus**.

car
bus

Where People Live

Many people live in cities.

The cities are big.

People live close to one another.

city

Other people live in towns.

The towns are small.

Fewer people live in them.

town

Things to See

I visit a state park.

I walk through a **forest**.

I see a **lake**.

forest
lake

I visit the capital.

This city is the state's main city.

People here make laws for
the state.

Glossary

bus

forest

car

lake

Index